ALL ABOUT
HANUKKAH

by
Judyth Groner
Madeline Wikler

Illustrated by
Kinny Kreiswirth

KAR-BEN
PUBLISHING

KAR-BEN PUBLISHING
A division of Lerner Publishing Group, Inc.
241 First Avenue North
Minneapolis, MN 55401 U.S.A.

Website address: www.karben.com

Library of Congress Cataloging-in-Publication Data

Groner, Judyth.
    All About Hanukkah / Judyth Groner and Madeline Wikler; illustrated by Kinny Kreiswirth
        p.   cm.
    Summary: Discusses the historical background for Hanukkah and examines its blessings, music, games, and modern observance.
        ISBN-13: 978-1-58013-051-6 (pbk. : alk. paper)
        1. Hanukkah—Juvenile literature. [1. Hanukkah.] I. Wikler, Madeline, 1943–
II. Kreiswirth, Kinney, ill. III. Title.
BM695.H3G68 1988
296.4'35—dc19   88-13435

Manufactured in the United States of America
5 6 7 8 9 10 – DP – 13 12 11 10 09 08

THE STORY OF HANUKKAH

Hanukkah was first celebrated over 2,000 years ago. The Jewish people were living in the land of Israel, which in those days was called Judea. Its capital and most holy city was Jerusalem. For many years, the Jews worked hard to build a beautiful Temple there. On Shabbat and the festivals, they came to the Temple to pray. They brought baskets filled with fruit and other gifts and put them on the Temple altar.

The Jews of Judea were not free. They were ruled by the kings of nearby Syria. For a time, these rulers let the Jews pray to God, celebrate the Jewish holidays, and follow the laws of the Torah.

Then a cruel king, Antiochus, came to power. He followed the Greek religion, and wanted everyone to believe as he did.

The Greeks of long ago worshipped many gods. They believed there was a god who made the sun shine, another who made the flowers grow, and still others who made it rain and thunder. They believed they knew what their gods looked like, and built statues called idols in their homes and temples.

The Jews believed then, as they do now, in one God. They believe that you cannot see God, and that you cannot build statues or draw pictures of what you think God looks like. The Jews refused to follow the Greek religion.

Antiochus expected everyone to obey him. He sent messengers to all the cities of Judea ordering the Jews to change their names to Greek names, wear Greek clothes, and eat Greek foods. He ordered them to put Greek idols in front of their homes and pray to them.

Some Jews obeyed the king's orders because they were afraid to be different. But many refused.

Antiochus was very angry at the Jews who would not change. He ordered his soldiers to march into Jerusalem. They destroyed homes and set fires in the streets. They stormed the Temple and tore down the Holy Ark. They built a Greek idol and put it on the Temple altar.

Many Jews were killed. Others took shelter in nearby villages. The soldiers went from town to town making sure the king's orders were being followed.

One day they came to Modi'in, a town not far from Jerusalem. They built an idol in the marketplace and called the Jews together to pray to it. The town leader, Mattathias, refused to bow down to the idol. He raised his sword and turned to the people of Modi'in. He told them he would continue to believe in One God and obey the laws of the Torah. He called on the Jews to follow him.

Mattathias, his five sons, and many of the Jews fought off the soldiers and escaped to the nearby mountains. They knew that to be free they would have to defeat the king and his army.

But Mattathias was old and sick. Before he died, he gathered his sons — Yohanan, Simon, Judah, Eliezer, and Jonathan — and blessed them. "*Hazak v'amatz*," he said to them in Hebrew. "Be strong and brave."

Mattathias appointed his son Judah to be the new leader. Judah was called *Maccabee*, which means hammer, and his followers became known as the Maccabees.

It was hard for Judah to form an army. The Jews were farmers, shepherds, and teachers. They were not trained to be soldiers. They had no uniforms and few weapons.

But the Maccabees knew the hills, caves, and countryside of Judea. They could move quickly and were able to surprise the king's army, even at night. Most important they were fighting for something they believed in. Their love for freedom gave them courage, and they fought long and hard.

The Maccabees went from village to village, defeating the Syrians and taking their weapons and uniforms. King Antiochus sent more and more soldiers, but the Jews drove them away.

Finally, the Maccabees reached Jerusalem. They went first to the Holy Temple. Its walls were crumbling. Weeds were growing in the courtyards. A Greek idol stood on the altar.

The Jewish fighters became builders. They scrubbed and polished the stone walls, cleaned the courtyards, and planted new trees. They took away the idols and built a new altar. They found iron spikes and put small torches on them to make a menorah. At last they were ready to celebrate.

On the 25th day of the
Hebrew month of Kislev,
exactly three years after the Syrian
soldiers destroyed Jerusalem, the Jews
lit the menorah and rededicated the Temple.
For eight days they celebrated joyfully. The
Maccabees proclaimed that every year the Jews should
celebrate a holiday of rededication, now called Hanukkah.

HANUKKAH TODAY

According to legend, when the Maccabees searched for the pure oil needed to light the Temple menorah, they found only one jug, enough to burn for just one day. But the oil lasted and lasted, and the menorah burned brightly for eight days.

Today, all over the world, Jewish families gather every year to celebrate the victory of the brave Maccabees. They light and bless the festive candles, exchange gifts, and retell the story of the little jug of oil.

In Israel, Hanukkah menorahs shine from the courtyards and rooftops of schools, synagogues, and office buildings, growing brighter each night as another light is added. In Modi'in, the ancient home of the Maccabees, torches are lit and carried to cities and villages throughout the land.

CANDLE-LIGHTING

The Hanukkah menorah — called a *hanukkiah* — should be lit after sunset and placed near a window, so that people passing by can see the lights. Hanukkah candles may be used only for enjoyment, so a *shamash*, a helper candle, is used to light the others. You should not do any work (not even homework!) while the lights are burning. Just relax and have fun. In some families, everyone lights his or her own *hanukkiah*. In other families, children and parents take turns lighting the candles.

On the first night, the *shamash* plus one candle are lit, on the second night the *shamash* plus two, and so on. You will need 44 candles for all eight nights. Candles should be lined up from right to left. But the last candle added is the first lit, and the lighting continues from left to right.

On Friday night Hanukkah candles are lit before Shabbat candles; on Saturday night, Hanukkah candles are lit after Havdalah.

CANDLE BLESSINGS

We say two blessings each night when we light the Hanukkah candles:

בָּרוּךְ אַתָּה יְיָ אֱלֹהֵינוּ מֶלֶךְ הָעוֹלָם,
אֲשֶׁר קִדְּשָׁנוּ בְּמִצְוֹתָיו וְצִוָּנוּ לְהַדְלִיק נֵר שֶׁל חֲנֻכָּה.

Baruch Atah Adonai Eloheinu Melech ha'olam, asher kid'shanu b'mitzvotav v'tzivanu l'hadlik ner shel Hanukkah.

We praise You, Adonai our God, Ruler of the Universe, Who makes us holy by Your mitzvot and commands us to light the Hanukkah candles.

בָּרוּךְ אַתָּה יְיָ אֱלֹהֵינוּ מֶלֶךְ הָעוֹלָם,
שֶׁעָשָׂה נִסִּים לַאֲבוֹתֵינוּ בַּיָּמִים הָהֵם. בַּזְּמַן הַזֶּה.

Baruch Atah Adonai Eloheinu Melech ha'olam, she'asah nisim la'avoteinu bayamim hahem baz'man hazeh.

We praise you, Adonai our God, Ruler of the Universe, for the miracles which You performed for our ancestors in those days.

On the first night we add this blessing:

בָּרוּךְ אַתָּה יְיָ אֱלֹהֵינוּ מֶלֶךְ הָעוֹלָם
שֶׁהֶחֱיָנוּ וְקִיְּמָנוּ וְהִגִּיעָנוּ לַזְּמַן הַזֶּה.

Baruch Atah Adonai Eloheinu Melech ha'olam, shehecheyanu, v'kiyemanu, v'higi'anu laz'man hazeh.

We praise You, Adonai our God, Ruler of the Universe, Who kept us alive and well to celebrate this special time.

Each night after the candles are lit, we say:

These Hanukkah lights are for us to enjoy. May their glow awaken us to give thanks for God's wondrous acts of deliverance.

Many families follow with the singing of Ma'Oz Tzur (Rock of Ages) and other Hanukkah songs.

FREE TO BE

The Maccabees rose up against King Antiochus because he would not let them live as Jews. Throughout history, Jews have been forced to flee countries where they were not allowed to practice their religion. Members of your family may have been among them.

Today, many people still struggle to live in freedom. Their governments do not permit them to come and go as they wish, or to observe their religious and national holidays.

While the candles are burning:

- Trace you family's geography. Were there times when they emigrated in search of freedom?

- Hanukkah was a struggle for spiritual freeedom; Purim was a struggle for physical survival. How are they different?

- Some families light an extra menorah to recall Jews living in fear, in poverty, and hunger who cannot celebrate Hanukkah.

FREE TO BE DIFFERENT

When King Antiochus ordered the Jews to believe in the Greek religion, many obeyed because they were afraid to be different. But the Maccabees believed it was wrong to copy another people.

Being Jewish today means being different. Jews celebrate Shabbat and Jewish holidays at home and in the synagogue. Non-Jews pray in churches and celebrate different holidays.

Christmas, a major Christian holiday, is celebrated around the time of Hanukkah. Because there are many Christians, we notice Christmas a lot — in homes, shopping centers, on television, and even in schools. At Christmas time especially, it can be hard for a Jewish person to be different.

While the candles are burning:

- Did you ever wish you weren't different?
- Have you ever talked with friends and classmates about Jewish history and holidays?
- How do differences enrich our community?
- Have you ever been singled out because you were Jewish? How did you handle the situation?

LEGENDS

Before books, stories were passed down from generation to generation. As they were retold, things were added, changed or forgotten.

When the story of Hanukkah was written down, years after it happened, different versions were recorded and many reasons were given for why we celebrate the holiday for eight days:

The jug of oil which should have burned for only one day burned for eight.

The Maccabees were so busy fighting the Syrians they had no time to celebrate Sukkot. After they rededicated the Temple, they celebrated Sukkot for the usual eight days.

To replace the Temple menorah which had been destroyed, the Maccabees gathered eight iron spikes which they lit for the celebration.

While the candles are burning:

- Does it matter whether the legends are true?

- What legends have been created in modern times to explain history for us?

- Midrash is a collection of legends which "fill in the gaps" in Bible stories. Pick a favorite story and create your own midrash.

MiRACLES

The four letters on the dreidel stand for the saying "A great miracle happened there."

A miracle is a wonderful happening we don't expect. Many miracles seem to contradict the laws of nature.

What miracles do we celebrate on Hanukkah?

First, even though the Maccabees were a very small army with few weapons, they were able to win over the large, well-trained Syrian army.

Second, the story is told that when the Maccabees were ready to light the menorah, they found only one jug of pure oil, enough to burn for a single day. But the oil burned for eight days.

Wonderful, unexpected things happen in our day, too.

While the candles are burning:

- How are the creation of the State of Israel, the rescue of Ethiopian Jewry, and the rebirth of Jewish life in the former Soviet Union modern day miracles?

- Why do we like to believe in miracles?

- Why do we enjoy reading about and watching superheroes?

ḤEROES

When the king's soldiers built an idol in the marketplace of Modi'in, the town leader Mattathias refused to bow down before it. He told the Jews he would continue to believe in One God and obey the laws of the Torah. He called on them to follow him into battle.

Before Mattathias died, he appointed his son Judah to be the new leader. It was said that "Judah struck with the force of a mighty hammer," which is how he got the name Maccabee, meaning hammer.

Both Mattathias and Judah are considered to be heroes.

While the candles are burning:

- What qualities define a hero?
- Who are the people you consider heroes and heroines in our day?
- Do you have to be "famous" to be a hero or heroine?
- Have you ever done anything "heroic"?

REBUILDING

When the Maccabees reached Jerusalem, they found the Temple in disrepair. They scrubbed and polished, cleaned and painted. Only then were they ready to dedicate the Temple and celebrate.

Hanukkah reminds us of our responsibility for *tikkun olam* (repairing the world). There are many ways we can fix things that are broken and help people whose lives have been broken.

While the candles are burning:

- Are there schools or playgrounds in your community that need cleaning and fixing? How can you help?

- Do you have used clothes, toys, and books in good condition that would be recycled and donated to families in need?

- What other projects can you think of for *tikkun olam*?

FAMILIES

The heroes of the Hanukkah story were Mattathias and his five sons. Judah needed the support of his brothers to stand up to the Syrians. Families help make our happy times sweeter and give us strength in difficult times.

Years ago, many people lived with, or near, grandparents and other relatives. Today families are often scattered. Hanukkah and other holidays are opportunities to get together.

While the candles are burning:

- How many relatives can you name? Who is the oldest and who is the youngest? Who lives the farthest away?

- What things do you enjoy doing with your family?

- How did your parents celebrate Hanukkah? Was it different from the way you celebrate?

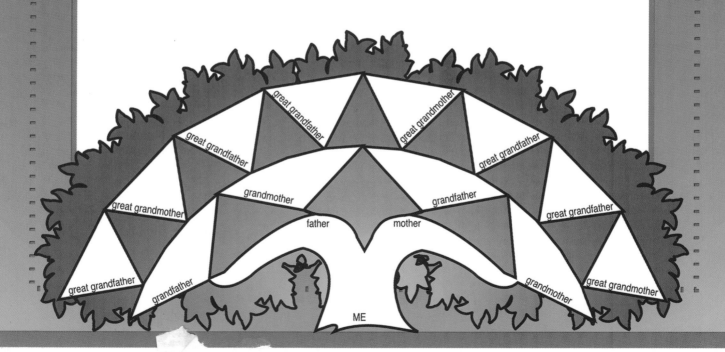

GiFTS, GELT AND GiViNG

Hanukkah *gelt*, the traditional holiday gift, recalls the coins minted by the Jewish state after the Maccabee victory. Today many families exchange gifts as well.

While it is fun to receive gifts, it is thoughtful to give them to those we love. Homemade cookies, photographs, and crafts are special, because they show you took the time to make them yourself. Another welcome gift is a promise to do something helpful — babysit, read to a friend, or run an errand. Hanukkah is also a time for *tzedakah* — helping those in need.

While the candles are burning:

- What can you do this week to bring Hanukkah joy to someone who is sick or lonely?

- Plan to set aside some of your Hanukkah gelt for tzedakah. Whom do you plan to give it to and why?

DREIDEL

Dreidel, the most popular Hanukkah game, is played with a spinning top. Dreidel in Yiddish means "turn," as does its Hebrew name, *sivivon*. There are four letters on the dreidel:

NUN GIMMEL HEY SHIN

They stand for the words *Nes Gadol Hayah Sham,* "A Great Miracle Happened There."

Dreidels in Israel have these letters:

NUN GIMMEL HEY PEY

They stand for *Nes Gadol Hayah Po,* "A Great Miracle Happened Here."

RULES FOR PLAYING

Give each player an equal number of nuts, raisins, or Hanukkah gelt. Each player puts one in the middle. The first player spins the dreidel. If it lands on:

> **N**un — Do **N**othing
> **G**immel — **G**et all
> **H**ey — Take **H**alf
> **S**hin (**P**ey) — **S**hare (**P**ut) one in

Before the next player spins, everyone must put in another piece.

DREIDEL VARIATIONS

♦ See who can keep a dreidel spinning the longest. Use a stop watch.

♦ Try spinning the dreidel upside down.

♦ Let each player spin a dreidel at the same time. Those whose dreidels land on the same letter get a point. Play to a specified number of points.

♦ Hebrew letters stand for numbers: Nun is 50, Gimmel is 3, Hey is 5, Shin is 300 and Pey is 80. Take turns spinning the dreidel, and record each player's score. See who can get to 1,000 first.

♦ Dreidel hunt: One player leaves the room while the others hide a dreidel. When the player returns to hunt for the hidden dreidel, the rest sing a Hanukkah song. As the searcher comes closer, the singing should get louder. See how long it takes each player to find the dreidel.

HANUKKAH RECIPES

On Hanukkah, it is customary to eat latkes (*levivot* in Hebrew) and jelly doughnuts (*sufganiyot*). Both are fried in oil and remind us of the miracle of the jug of oil that burned for eight days.

POTATO LATKES
(LEVIVOT)

2 c. grated potatoes
small onion
2 eggs

2 Tbsp. flour or matzah meal
1 tsp. salt
oil for frying

Grate potatoes and onion and place in a bowl. Add the eggs, salt, and meal. Drain off excess liquid. Drop by spoonfuls into well-oiled frying pan. Fry on both sides in hot oil. Serve with applesauce or sour cream.

DOUGHNUTS
(SUFGANIYOT)

¾ cup orange juice/water
¼ lb. margarine
4 Tbsp. sugar
2 pkg. yeast

3 cups flour
2 eggs, beaten
Dash of salt
Powdered sugar/cinnamon

Combine juice, margarine, and sugar and heat until margarine melts. Cool to lukewarm and add yeast. Stir until dissolved. Combine all ingredients and mix. Knead until smooth, adding more flour if necessary. Place dough in greased bowl, cover, and let rise for thirty minutes. Punch down. Shape small pieces of dough into balls, rings, or braids. Cover. Let rise another thirty minutes. Deep fry in hot oil. Drain. Put a few teaspoons of powdered sugar and cinnamon in a paper bag. Add doughnuts and shake.

REMINDER: *Cooking with hot oil can be very dangerous. Make sure that a grown-up is helping you.*

CANDLE BLESSINGS

Traditional

Music Arranged by Sue Roemer

MA'OZ TZUR

Traditional

Ma - oz tzur ye shu - a - ti, L'cha - na - eh l' - sha be - ach.
Rock of a - ges, let our song Praise Thy sav - ing — pow - er;

Ti - kon beit te - fi - la - ti v'sham to - dah ne - za be - ach.
Thou a - midst the rag - ing foes Wast our shelt' - ring — tow - er.

Le - eit ta - chin mat - be - ach mi - tzar ham - na be - ach,
Fu - rious they as - sailed us, But Thine arm a - vailed _____ us,

Az eg - mor be - shir miz - mor, Cha - nu - kat ha - miz be - ach.
And Thy word — broke their sword — When our own strength failed — us.

Az eg - mor be - shir miz - mor, Cha - nu - kat ha - miz be - ach.
And Thy word — broke their sword — When our own strength failed — us.

CHANUKAH, OH CHANUKAH

Yiddish: M. Riversman
Hebrew: A. Evronim

FOLK SONG

Oh Cha-nu-kah, Oh Cha-nu-kah, come light the me-no-rah___, Lets___ have a par - ty, we'll all dance the ho - rah. Ga-ther round the ta - ble, we'll give you a treat: Drei - dels to play with and lat-kes to eat. And while we are play-ing, The can-dles are burn-ing___ low. One for each night, they will shed a sweet light to re-

1. mind us of days long a - go___.

2. mind us of days long a - go.

Oy Chanukah, Oy Chanukah,
A yom tov a sheyner.
A lustiger, a frelacher nito noch a zoyner.
Alle nacht in dreidlach shpiln mir.
Zudig heyse latkes essen on a shir.
Geshvinder tzindt kinder
Di dinike lichtecha ohn.
Zogt "Al hanisim," loibt Gott far di nisim
Un kumt gicher tantzen in kohn.

Yemei ha-Chanukah,
Chanukat mikdashenu
Begil uv'simchah
Mimalim et libenu.
Laila vayom s'vivonenu yisov.
Sufganiyot nochal bam larov.
Ha'iru hadliku nerot Chanukah rabim.
Al hanisim v'al hanifla'ot
Asher cholelu ha-Maccabim.